Little People, **BIG DREAMS**®

ROSA PARKS

Little People, BIG DREAMS®
ROSA PARKS

Written by
Lisbeth Kaiser

Illustrated by
Marta Antelo

Frances Lincoln
Children's Books

Rosa grew up near Montgomery, Alabama, with her mother, brother and grandparents.

She was very little and very brave, and she always tried to do what was right.

When she was young, Rosa's grandparents told her stories about slavery, when black people weren't free to live like other people.

Slavery was over, but times were still hard for Rosa and her family. Black people were treated very badly and told they were not equal to white people.

Every day, Rosa watched the school bus go by taking white children to their big school. It didn't stop for her. She had to walk a long way to the one-room school that was just for black children.

Rosa knew this wasn't right. She knew she was a regular person, just as good as anyone else.

Lots of times, she had to make sure other people knew it too.

When Rosa grew up and got a job in the city, she couldn't use the same doors, lifts, bathrooms or water fountains as white people.

She could ride the bus, but she had to sit at the back. Her life was full of rules that she knew weren't right.

Rosa fell in love with a man named Raymond who was trying to change the rules to be more fair and equal.

Soon Rosa started working, too, trying to get more rights for black people and help for those who were treated badly. She worked day after day, even when it seemed like nothing would ever change.

On her way home from the city one day, a bus driver
told Rosa to stand up so a white person could take her
seat. She was sick of rules that she knew were wrong.
She thought, *enough*. She said, "No".

Rosa was taken to jail. She wasn't scared, because she knew that what she was fighting for was right.

When Rosa came home that night, she talked with her friends and family about what to do. She decided to keep fighting, no matter how hard it would be.

Black people all over the city heard what had happened to Rosa. They thought, *enough*.

Rosa inspired them to stop riding the buses until the rules changed.

So they walked, to school and to work and to the shops, in all kinds of weather.

Rosa travelled the country – from New York to San Francisco – to convince other people to join the fight.

Finally, after one year, the Supreme Court decided that treating black people differently from white people on buses was wrong. The rules were going to change!

It was no longer safe for Rosa to live in Alabama. She moved to Detroit and fought for fair schools, jobs and houses for black people.

We have to keep trying as long as we are alive

She fought for voting rights, women's rights and the rights of people in prison.

When Rosa was an older woman, she was given awards and told she was a hero. But she knew who she was.

A regular person, just as good as anyone else. And she had work to do.

ROSA PARKS

(Born 1913 • Died 2005)

c. 1950

1955

Rosa Parks was an American activist and one of the most important figures in the civil rights movement. The grandchild of former slaves, she grew up with her mother, brother and grandparents on a small farm outside of Montgomery, Alabama, where she faced mean and unfair treatment because of her skin colour. She regularly resisted with bravery and dignity. It wasn't until she met her husband, Raymond Parks, that she learned about activism. At 30, she became a leader in the National Association for the Advancement of Coloured People (NAACP) in Montgomery and began working to end inequality.

1965   1984

When she was 42, Rosa was taken from a bus and jailed because she refused to give her seat to a white person. Her arrest brought the black people of Montgomery together to demand change and she helped lead them in a year-long boycott of the buses. Rosa's actions and hard work helped establish the civil rights movement. They also cost her family their jobs and safety. They moved north to Detroit, where Rosa was dismayed to find that great inequality persisted. She remained an activist for the rest of her life, helping many people and inspiring countless others with her bravery, dignity and determination in the ongoing fight for human equality.

Want to find out more about **Rosa Parks**?

She has written a book about her life:

I am Rosa Parks by Rosa Parks and James Haskins

You could also try these:

I am Rosa Parks by Brad Meltzer

Who Was Rosa Parks? by Yona Zeldis McDonough

And if you're near the Henry Ford Museum in Michigan, you could even visit the famous Rosa Parks bus.

Brimming with creative inspiration, how-to projects, and useful information to enrich your everyday life, quarto.com is a favourite destination for those pursuing their interests and passions.

Text copyright © 2017 Lisbeth Kaiser. Illustrations copyright © 2017 Marta Antelo.
Original concept of the series by Maria Isabel Sánchez Vegara, published by Alba Editorial, S.L.U.
"Little People, BIG DREAMS" and "Pequeña & Grande" are trademarks of Alba Editorial S.L.U. and/or Beautifool Couple S.L.
First published in the UK in 2017 by Frances Lincoln Children's Books,
an imprint of The Quarto Group, The Old Brewery, 6 Blundell Street, London N7 9BH
The Old Brewery, 6 Blundell Street, London N7 9BH, UK.
T (0)20 7700 6700 **www.Quarto.com**

ISBN: 978-1-78603-017-7

Published by Rachel Williams • Designed by Karissa Santos
Edited by Katy Flint • Production by Kate O'Riordan

Manufactured in Guangdong, China CC122022

17

Photographic acknowledgements (pages 28-29, from left to right) 1. Rosa Parks Collection at the Library of Congress, 2015 © The Washington Post, Getty Images 2. Rosa Louise McCauley Parks booking photo, 1955 © Universal Images Group, Getty Images 3. Selma to Montgomery March, 1965 © Stephen F. Somerstein, Getty Images 4. Rosa Parks protesting apartheid, 1984 © Bettman, Getty Images

Collect the *Little People,* **BIG DREAMS®** series:

FRIDA KAHLO 	**COCO CHANEL**	**MAYA ANGELOU** 	**AMELIA EARHART** 	**AGATHA CHRISTIE** 	**MARIE CURIE** 	**ROSA PARKS**	**AUDREY HEPBURN**

EMMELINE PANKHURST 	**ELLA FITZGERALD** 	**ADA LOVELACE** 	**JANE AUSTEN** 	**GEORGIA O'KEEFFE**	**HARRIET TUBMAN** 	**ANNE FRANK** 	**MOTHER TERESA**

JOSEPHINE BAKER 	**L. M. MONTGOMERY** 	**JANE GOODALL** 	**SIMONE DE BEAUVOIR** 	**MUHAMMAD ALI** 	**STEPHEN HAWKING** 	**MARIA MONTESSORI** 	**VIVIENNE WESTWOOD**

MAHATMA GANDHI 	**DAVID BOWIE** 	**WILMA RUDOLPH** 	**DOLLY PARTON** 	**BRUCE LEE** 	**RUDOLF NUREYEV** 	**ZAHA HADID** 	**MARY SHELLEY**

MARTIN LUTHER KING JR. 	**DAVID ATTENBOROUGH**	**ASTRID LINDGREN** 	**EVONNE GOOLAGONG** 	**BOB DYLAN** 	**ALAN TURING** 	**BILLIE JEAN KING** 	**GRETA THUNBERG**

JESSE OWENS	**JEAN-MICHEL BASQUIAT** 	**ARETHA FRANKLIN** 	**CORAZON AQUINO** 	**PELÉ** 	**ERNEST SHACKLETON** 	**STEVE JOBS** 	**AYRTON SENNA**

LOUISE BOURGEOIS 	**ELTON JOHN** 	**JOHN LENNON** 	**PRINCE** 	**CHARLES DARWIN** 	**CAPTAIN TOM MOORE** 	**HANS CHRISTIAN ANDERSEN**	**STEVIE WONDER** 

MEGAN RAPINOE

MARY ANNING

MALALA YOUSAFZAI

ANDY WARHOL

RUPAUL

MICHELLE OBAMA

MINDY KALING

IRIS APFEL

ROSALIND FRANKLIN

RUTH BADER GINSBURG

MARILYN MONROE

KAMALA HARRIS

ALBERT EINSTEIN

CHARLES DICKENS

YOKO ONO

MICHAEL JORDAN

NELSON MANDELA

PABLO PICASSO

AMANDA GORMAN

GLORIA STEINEM

FLORENCE NIGHTINGALE

HARRY HOUDINI

J.R.R. TOLKIEN

ELVIS PRESLEY

NEIL ARMSTRONG

ALEXANDER VON HUMBOLDT

NIKOLA TESLA

WILMA MANKILLER

MARCUS RASHFORD

LAVERNE COX

MAE JEMISON

DWAYNE JOHNSON

HELEN KELLER
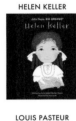

ANNA PAVLOVA

QUEEN ELIZABETH

TERRY FOX

HEDY LAMARR

SHAKIRA

FREDDIE MERCURY

LEWIS HAMILTON

LOUIS PASTEUR

PRINCESS DIANA

DAVID HOCKNEY

VANESSA NAKATE

Scan the QR code for free activity sheets, teachers' notes and more information about the series at www.littlepeoplebigdreams.com